D1541019

Sadri Returns to Bali

A tale of the Balinese Galungan festival

Elisabeth Waldmeier

PERIPLUS

Published by Periplus Editions (HK) Ltd

Copyright © 2002 Elisabeth Waldmeier

All rights reserved.

No part of this publication may be reproduced, stored in a retrieval system or transmitted in any form or by any means, electronic, mechanical, photocopying, recording or otherwise without prior permission of the publisher.

ISBN 0-7946-0053-0

Printed in Singapore

Translator: Susan Tuttle-Laube
Editors: Liana Romulo, Kim Inglis, Jocelyn Lau
Designer: Ming Pang

Distributed by:

North America, Latin America & Europe
Tuttle Publishing, Distribution Center,
Airport Industrial Park, 364 Innovation Drive,
North Clarendon, VT 05759-9436, USA
Tel (802) 773 8930; fax (802) 773 6993

Asia Pacific
Berkeley Books Pte Ltd, 130 Joo Seng Road #06-01/03,
Singapore 368357, Singapore
Tel (65) 6280 3320; fax (65) 6280 6290

Japan & Korea
Tuttle Publishing, Yaekari Building, 3rd Floor,
5-4-12 Osaki, Shinagawa-ku
Tokyo 141-0032, Japan
Tel (81-3) 5437 0171; fax (81-3) 5437 0755

Indonesia
PT Java Books Indonesia, PT Jl Kelapa Gading Kirana,
Blok A14 No 17, Jakarta 14240, Indonesia
Tel (62-21) 451 5351; fax (62-21) 453 4987

08 07 06 05 04 03
7 6 5 4 3 2

Foreword

On Bali every 210 days, a lavish ten-day celebration known as Galungan takes place. With feasts, offerings, and prayer, Balinese Hindus honor their Gods, deified ancestors, and departed souls, and appease the demons and evil spirits that may lurk in the villages.

Based on this Balinese festival, and set in a world where invisible presences co-exist with—and are as much a reality as—human beings, Elisabeth Waldmeier has written an enchanting tale about Sadri. This small, lovable ancestral spirit revisits his former home and guides us through a traditional Bali of bustling marketplace activities, lush rice fields, unceasing Galungan preparations, and the exhilarating finale—open-air stage performances.

For the sake of our children, let's hope the old world of customs and traditions, and of tales and storytelling will never disappear.

Dr. Urs Ramseyer
Curator, Indonesian Department
Museum of the Cultures
Basel, Switzerland

"*Koo-koo-roo-koo-koo*!" The familiar sound of crowing roosters gently woke Sadri from his sleep. He quickly got up from his sleeping mat and dressed with extra care, wrapping his best *kambèn* around his hips and tucking a perfect red hibiscus blossom behind his ear. For today was a special day, Sadri knew. It was the first day of Galungan, and for ten whole days everyone on the island of Bali would be honoring their gods and ancestors.

Sadri was very excited. He was one of the ancestral spirits that were specially invited to the celebrations. Indeed, the people of Bali would be paying their respects to him!

The sky was just beginning to lighten by the time Sadri arrived at the small village he visited every two hundred and ten days for the festival. At the entrance Sadri paused for a moment to look at the *pènjor*—tall arching bamboo poles with their *janur* offerings—lining both sides of the dirt path. He smiled as a warm feeling washed over him. The people of the village had put up these offerings to let Sadri know that he was welcome, as they did every Galungan.

Sadri slowly made his way down the path, taking in the familiar scenes: thatched roof houses surrounded by lush green plants, trees heavy with papayas,

mangoes, bananas, coconuts, and many other tropical fruits. And, best of all, laid out at the entryways of every home were food offerings, beautifully presented on palm leaves.

"Oh!" Sadri exclaimed. "My people here on Bali are so kind. They've left me so much to eat."

He sat on the steps leading into one of the homes, savoring the sweet aroma of the food around him. Then he began sampling the feast of steamed rice, dried fish, and fresh fruit. With every bite, pure happiness seemed to fill him, and before long he could not eat any more.

Leaving plenty of food behind, Sadri decided it was time to pay a visit to the home that he once lived in many, many years ago, before he became a spirit. The people that lived in it now were his descendants, and they were waiting to pay their respects to him.

Quietly, Sadri slipped into the garden of his former home. Even though he was invisible to humans, he did not want to startle anyone by making any loud noises. He glanced around, looking out for the family he had grown to love over the years—the two young sisters, Made and Nyoman; their older brother, Wayan; their baby brother, Ketut; their parents, Mother Ranis and Father Merta; and their silver-haired grandmother.

Soon Sadri heard the swishing sound of a *sampat*, a coarse broom of long twigs tied together.

"That must be Grandmother!" he thought. She always swept the garden very early in the morning. Stepping out from behind a hibiscus plant, Sadri saw Grandmother, with Mother Ranis close by. Grandmother was indeed sweeping the compound with the *sampat*, and Mother Ranis was carrying a basketful of food offerings to the shrine.

He pressed his palms together in a gesture of greeting. "*Nunas lugra*," he whispered, asking for permission to enter the house.

Sadri heard laughter coming from inside the house. "The girls," he thought, eager to see them. He could also hear little Ketut crying, along with the clattering sounds of pots and pans.

Then a deep voice spoke over all the noise. "Sadri will come today!"

It was Father Merta's voice, which made Sadri so excited that he bounded up the stairs rather clumsily, nearly knocking over an oil lamp. Immediately the girls stopped laughing, and even baby Ketut fell silent. They sensed that Sadri had arrived.

After a moment, Father Merta spoke again. "Sadri," he said, his kind eyes sparkling, "we greet you. In your honor we have decorated the shrine with the best cloths, and we have prepared the most delicious foods for you to taste. Today we will remember you and tell each other stories about how remarkable you were."

Sadri's heart filled with emotion. It felt wonderful to be remembered, but at the same time he wished he were more than just a memory.

The next afternoon Sadri took a long walk out to the paddy fields, where the rice goddess, Déwi Sri, lived. He wanted to thank her for giving the Balinese people plenty of rice to eat. Sadri knew that the rice the goddess provided so abundantly kept the Balinese healthy and happy.

He walked carefully along the narrow mud paths between rice paddies, listening for her voice. The setting sun reflected off the shallow waters of the fields on either side of him. Soon he could hear a sweet melody just beneath the soft whispering of the wind.

"Déwi Sri," he called out. "I am here!"

Sadri listened intently, walking in the direction of the faint song. Gradually the goddess's singing became more and more distinct, and Sadri came upon a small bamboo hut set in the fields. Sadri knew the rice goddess often watched over her crops from here.

"Déwi Sri," Sadri said, approaching the little hut, "dance with me! You are the most generous of all goddesses, and I know your harvest will be extremely abundant this year."

All around him, ten thousand stalks of rice began to sway gently back and forth, sending ripples across the green fields. These thin, reedy rice plants were Déwi Sri's children. Sadri watched them dance for several minutes, marveling at their grace, and then he began to move along with them. Looking up at the fast darkening sky and feeling the warm night air against his face, Sadri opened his arms wide and let the wind and the music take him.

Back and forth he swayed, shouting joyously, "Dance with me, goddesss Déwi Sri! Dance! Let's celebrate your harvest!"

On the fifth day Sadri thought it would be a good idea to visit the village market, which was located in the village square. It was an especially warm day, and he thought it might be pleasant to sit in the cool shade of the giant *waringin* tree, which had a nice view of the marketplace.

The *waringin* towered majestically over the market, its thick, twisting roots hanging from its branches as vines would. Just by looking at it Sadri could feel its strength and holiness.

Sadri slowly made his way to the tree, passing many fruit and vegetable stands, and vendors selling different foods. Then, taking hold of one of the tree's ropelike roots, he swung up into the tree, where there was a small bamboo house nestled among the leaves. Sadri used to come to this tree house a long time ago, and he knew that the Balinese had built it as a special home for the drum *kulkul*.

Perched high up in the tree, Sadri could now watch all the activity going on. He could even smell the pungent odor of the durian fruits, and listen to the conversations below.

"I'll give you two hundred rupiah for this," a woman haggled, after tasting a bit of durian.

The vendor shook his head. "No, five hundred," he said, holding up the large fruit. "This is the best durian in the market. It's very rich and creamy."

"Four hundred," the woman said, holding out a fistful of rupiah. "I know it's delicious, but I don't have any more money with me."

The vendor laughed good-naturedly. "Well, then. Four hundred will do."

Grinning, the woman placed the durian in her basket. Sadri noticed that it was already filled with mandarin oranges, heads of cabbage, onions, duck eggs, and fish.

"This is such a wonderful, peaceful place," Sadri thought dreamily. "It's like paradise!" He loved Bali so much that he wished he could stay and live there, but he knew his visit would soon be coming to an end. *Sanghyang Widi*, the Almighty, would be calling him back in just a few days.

All too soon the final day of Galungan arrived. Mother Ranis and the other women in the village had been baking colorful rice cakes and weaving elaborate ornaments out of palm leaves. Father Merta, too, had been busy practicing his drumming, as he was going to beat the drum at the celebration. But Sadri was particularly excited about watching Wayan's performance. Wayan was a *baris* dancer, and tonight, for the first time, he would dance for the gods.

By nightfall the air was filled with energy and excitement. Sadri walked briskly among the crowd, trying to find his family. All around him people were dressed in their finest clothes—the men had special coverings on their heads, and the women wore flowers in their hair. Everyone was in a merry mood, laughing, eating, and even dancing.

Finally he spotted Made and Nyoman, who were happily snacking on *jaja*, or colorful rice cakes. Not far from them was Grandmother, cradling little Ketut in her arms. He also saw Mother Ranis chatting with some other women, but Father Merta and Wayan were not there. Sadri guessed they were preparing for the performance, and praying to the gods for a successful show.

Suddenly a crowd nearby began shouting and clapping their hands. Sadri rushed forward to get a better view. On a wall made of cloth, a *wayang kulit* or shadow puppet show had just begun. It was one of his favorite shadow plays, about Hanuman, the monkey king! The puppets were so funny that many people stayed to watch the show. Sadri laughed and laughed until his stomach hurt.

Then, all at once, the thunderous *boom-boom-boom* of beating drums filled the air, and Wayan stepped into the village square. Sadri gasped. Adorned with makeup, an elaborate headdress, and a costume that sparkled with precious stones, Wayan looked like a bold and courageous warrior.

Sadri was completely mesmerized. As he took in every turn of Wayan's wrists, every graceful curl of his fingers and toes, and every flick of his eyes, Sadri's body began to move, too.

Sadri could not understand what was happening to him. It was as if a magical force had taken over his body, and was making him dance.

"Dance with him," a voice told him. "Dance in him!"

Sadri let himself go. The crowd around him seemed to fade into the distance, but Wayan and the beating drums filled his heart and body.

Sadri danced with all the energy and life in him. As he did, Wayan's movements seemed to become wilder and more passionate. It was as if Wayan were possessed with Sadri's spirit.

Someone in the crowd exclaimed: "He dances marvelously, like the great dancer Sadri once did!"

Before dawn the next day Sadri left the magical island of Bali. Galungan was now over, and it was time to return to the Almighty. But Sadri was not at all sad. Last night, as he danced, he was more than just a memory. He knew that his spirit lived on in Wayan.

Glossary

kambèn	Indonesian wrap-around skirt
pènjor	tall bamboo poles signifying festival
janur	decorations made from yellow coconut and young sago palm leaves, hung from *pènjor*
sampat	coarse broom of long twigs
nunas lugra	welcome greeting, requesting permission to enter
Déwi Sri	rice goddess (also goddess of fertility)
waringin	banyan tree, considered holy by the Balinese
kulkul	tubular wooden drum for signals
rupiah	Indonesian currency
Sanghyang Widi	the Almighty (God)
baris	warrior dance
jaja	colorful rice cakes
wayang kulit	puppet shadow play